Winter
SOLSTICE

Winter SOLSTICE

THE LOST WRITINGS OF ZORAK DE BORNEO

DAVID JOE RICHARDSON

WINTER SOLSTICE
THE LOST WRITINGS OF ZORAK DE BORNEO

iUniverse books may be ordered through booksellers or by contacting:

iUniverse
1663 Liberty Drive
Bloomington, IN 47403
www.iuniverse.com
844-349-9409

ISBN: 978-1-6632-6588-3 (sc)
ISBN: 978-1-6632-6589-0 (e)

Library of Congress Control Number: 2024916606

Print information available on the last page.

iUniverse rev. date: 09/05/2024

To my knowledge Zorak de Borneo has never assumed physical incarnation; he exists in my mind. The lost writings are products of his imagination: notes of a wandering soul from the late-20th and early-21st Centuries.

"Winter Solstice" is a collection which conveys the hope, despair, excitement and wonder of being lost; homage to the shortest day of the year from which point darkness inevitably succumbs to light.

David Joe Richardson
December 21, 2017

Cover Photo:
Village Graveyard,
Holzgerlingen, Germany
December 21, 2007

Table of Context

Mink, Glass, Mask!

Cumulative Clouds

Butterflies At Dawn

Mink, Glass, Mask!

Soiree on the Palace Grounds

Nocturnal incantations
Announce the sun's daily death
And the nightly call for the dead to dance.

Inclinations explode in my skull
In response your cryptic glance.
Torches flicker as a fugue begins.

You are an enchanted beast of northern taste
Among mirrors and mannequins;
You provoke an exuberant protuberance I long to share.

I'll dispense with dull formalities
If you will take a chance.
I may have a rare disease
And you may have this dance.

Don't say I didn't warn you!
Don't say I didn't warn you!
Don't say I didn't warn you!
May I have this dance?

Prelude:

I sat up in bed in the middle of the night and there was Man Ray. The illustrious painter, photographer, sculptor, largely known for his contributions to the Dada and Surrealist art movements, sat quietly by the open window. I don't know how long he had been there.

Then we were standing together at the edge of an indoor pool. The lights made the water sparkle as people splashed around fully clothed. The walls glowed greenish-blue. It was steamy but neither hot nor cold. I noticed that everyone, including us, wore white bathing caps.

"It looks like everybody is prepared for brain surgery," I heard myself say. But not a word was heard from Man Ray. Then he nodded and raised his left eyebrow as he smiled.
"Write me a poem."
And I said, "okay."

White porcelain came to mind. Man Ray's friend, Marcel Duchamp, submitted a piece for display at an exhibition of the American Society of Independent Artists in 1917. It was rejected. Ah, a poem to give this "ready-made" sculpture an opportunity to explain itself.

"How does this sound?" I heard myself say, but discovered that if anyone had been there they had since gone away. I said "good night" to no one in particular and I fell asleep.

I sat up that morning and at the foot of my bed was a piece of paper. On it, in a hand I didn't recognize, was a poem....

Ballad of R. Mutt

"My purpose void of sophistry, my life was simple; yes. And then there came Marcel Duchamp who saw my value best. I am a urinal. It's plain to

see. But, before you sally forth to pee, remember please my status now: a
work of art! Embracing the taste of the bourgeoisie!"

Thus with taste the fountain spake,
And spake again in haste...

    "Father? Father!
    "Trade your pants for leather glasses!
    "Stand erect among the masses!"

I lost my grip when I heard that voice,
Which echoed through the gilded hall.

    "My son? My son!
    "It can't be you!
    "My son is not that tall..."

    "It cannot be," the fountain said, "and yet it can be, too."
    "My status is debatable; and that is very true.
    "Who's to judge the measure of a man?
    "I'm positioned best to know -
    "If not me, then who?"

I felt disturbed as I pondered the words,
Tucking my junk away.
What is art? Who is to say?
The question still lingers.... both then and today.

Hamburger Helmut

He was an otherwise normal, civil servant in Hamburg.
However, he had always wondered how it would feel
To wear a hat of raw meat.

When he could withstand the mystery no longer,
He secretly bought some ground beef.
And took it home.

He quickly realized to get the full effect
He would need to shave his head.
So he did.

It was cool; literally as well as figuratively.
However, his wife discovered him,
And vigorously questioned his motivations.
She called him a meat-head.
He had to admit she was right.

Soon it was not enough to simply wear it;
He wanted to walk around in it.
He became popular with the neighborhood dogs.

He was once a civil servant without a cause;
But he took a pause
At the forbidden arcade where obsessions are obtained
And never forgotten.

Crispy Britches

Josephine stood at her cash register,
Ablaze in her sweet, crispy britches.

Copper or Bronze?
Or golden aluminum?
I haven't a clue
The actual color that her shanks are clad;
But I am glad, and grateful, too.
I am starting to think about things I need to do.

"Paper or plastic?"
"Oh, either will do…
"Thank you"

Shiny and bright, her face a slightly brushed,
Blushing hue:

You think she might be craving you,
In her sweet, crispy britches…

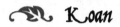 **Koan**

Dead guy wearing glasses

Fat guy in a skeleton costume

Skeleton wearing

Nothing

6

Ode to Modern Medicine

A stitch here, a snippet there:
Now I'm hung like a hippopotamus.
The donor wishes to remain anonymous.

ॐ Swallow with Care

"(Hey man), you're not going to eat that, are you?"

Irresistibly delicious
All knowledge would seem;
But knowledge too certain
Is questionable cuisine

"(Hey man), I don't think I'll eat that after all."

Belfast Sunset

Lines composed while pondering a pint of stout

The color and textures are sublime;
Light at the top, darkening as it settles across a sophisticated spectrum of
Black.
But first, the laws of physics engage in a minuet within the confines of a glass.

Stew arrives: Oh yeah!
Steam rises to the occasion,
Heralding an orgy of gigantic potatoes, carrots, and meat.

Now: a quaff.
Wow! Taste buds frolic in the froth of a wave of black cream.
I'm almost scared to blink for fear this moment will dissipate,
Or leave me for another's dream.

Red headed girl with a nose ring
Asks me if everything is all right.
Oh, yeah.
Yeah, It's all right.

Her hair is piled high on her head.
And although naturally red
She gave it a new hue--
Sort of crimson, instead of the
Auburn eyes peeping out from her roots.

She has a tattoo, as well.
I saw it
On her arm,
Across her bicep.
Otherwise she looks nothing like a sailor.

Another pint....

I threw my watch into Pearl Harbor.
The water gleamed beneath the evening lights
As time disappeared below.

And time stopped until I saw your face again.

In a tear-drop deep in my heart
I see your reflection.
Transported by memories -
I dive in when you are not near.
And I shed another tear.

Your re-assignment
May cause you consternation
Based upon unknown circumstances,
But your transfer will not be the basis
For administrative retraction.
Death is not a grieveable action.

Thus did decry
The great civil servant in the sky.

Boring Barracuda

Two guys who had too, too much to drink
And not enough to think –
Decided to play catch with a dead barracuda.

The barracuda was pretty boring,
Figuratively snoring.
However, it eventually managed to liven things up.

But not in a good way.

Just because you like it
Doesn't mean you're good at it

Just because you're not good at it
Doesn't mean you can't like it

Just because you can
Doesn't mean you should

Just because you should
Doesn't mean you shouldn't

Just because you shouldn't
Doesn't mean you shouldn't

Just because you shan't
Doesn't mean you can't

Just because you don't
Doesn't mean you wont

Just because you are meat
Doesn't make you a treat

Car exhaust and animal juices,
The city dies and reproduces.

"God is scarier than Satan,"
He thought to himself in a dark, back room at Club Hubba Hubba on
Hotel Street.
Seeing movement among the bodies on the floor,
He squeezed off another round:
Just in case.

He left the club as the band
Launched into their second set.
The streets were wet;
Dashing headlights made the rain
Look like a horizontal hail of bullets.

He stood on the street.
The hiss of cars merged with the sound of music just inside;
The clashes from the bowling alley next door
Sounded vaguely like waves crashing against the shore.
"Oceanfront property in the heart of downtown," he thought to himself.

His thoughts were broken by a question from one of his thug assistants:
"Hey boss, do you think Stonehenge was built by aliens?"
"Yeah, it was a fuck'n bowling alley."

Meanwhile, a chartered airplane
Crossed and re-crossed the international dateline
In an effort to keep his misinformed, billionaire mob-boss alive.

Helmut's Holiday

He relaxed in the chair in his underwear,
His hamburger helmet was cool and moist.
Feeling it starting to droop round the ears
He adjusted with a tender hoist;
His shaved head absorbed the meaty moisture eagerly,
But would it leave a stain?
And then he began to wonder about his brain.

Texture means a great deal. As does composition;
But you see, the size of the cranium will make that determination.
Where the burger meats the flesh—as it were—is how it feels:
Raw meat against the skin of your head. Meat? Of course, and very red.

Fall asleep in the barber's chair—it's a dare!
Dream about anything you choose and dream it well;
But before you embark on a tenderloin lark: beware!
A hamburger helmet casts a beefy, well-marbled spell.

Cumulative Clouds

The mystery is somehow sweet.
Children are drinking moonbeam tea
And smiling.

Celtic warriors emerge from the glade as
We watch from a car on a highway in Scotland.
The Beatles are singing "She Loves You," as we listen to the radio--
A young couple from Liverpool and me.
They picked me up while I was hitchhiking.
I tell them I'm an astral projectionist from Neptune, Kansas.
They chuckle nervously.

Saturday afternoon I got on a bus and sat next to an Italian guy who just
kissed his girlfriend goodbye. I don't know if they ever saw each other
again. He offered me a sandwich.

Early Sunday morning I left my sweatshirt on a milk truck bound for
Colchester. The milkman was a nice guy who extolled the virtues of
foreign travel. He told me about his German girlfriend. "She didn't speak
any English, and all I can say in German is 'Heil Hitler,'" he said with a
laugh. But I was given to understand they understood each other very well.

I remember dreaming I lost my mind
And I'm not sure if I ever found it
Because I think I woke up.

The mystery is somehow sweet.
Children are drinking moonbeam tea
And smiling.

Punting at Cambridge was never so glorious!
American tourists--
Oh, how they bore us,
With inane repartee
For which they're notorious.

Nicholas, Nicholas, do pass a jar,
And gaze at the bank where a maiden doth rest.
She smiles sans a clue as we look up her dress--
I'm losing control, what blissful distress!

Cardinal Woolsey, or was it the Pope?
In any event, the founder of this,
Lives on in my memory -- such as it is --
As an unseen provider...rather like soap!

Punting at Cambridge – or are we at Oxford?
We're American tourists and such details do bore us
As much as each other;
But today we are punting, and the English adore us!

Lady of the Fan

You wave
And leaves
Flicker in the brilliance of what was a windless summer day.

You unleash flames upon flesh
To feast like cannibal sharks
In savage oceans of distant moons.

You were born before me
Yet after me you shall live.
You rise above a field strewn with shards of the broken hourglass.

In a local Havana café
Old men play cards and drink rum
The way they did before, during, and after the revolution.

Above this smoky, smoldering scene
Churns a ceiling fan – unseen –
Slowly and sardonically;
As if not to defy,
But to verify
The heat.

Summer Solstice

Join me for a flagon of ale to watch the day recede
Into the rich warm night of mid-summer

The songs of the season are sung by cicadas
And the snorting of startled horses
As daylight slowly, ineluctably, succumbs

The eyes are weary but I cannot sleep
As long as I hear the children, birds, and sheep
Sharing a desire to prolong the day
With the gentle, sighing sun

Ode: To Nocturnal Economics

Through eyes within my throbbing head
I search the street where pleasures dwell.
Beneath the dismal lights of red
I crave heaven
In a scene from hell.

The marketplace!
The passion of the commodities exchange fills the air.
London! Tokyo! It could be anywhere.

An ancient rhythm beating fast, the timeless dance begins anew.
Although I know it cannot last, I'll forget the past -
At least until the night is through.

We are ponies off a carousel, temporarily set free
To feast upon the sweetness of a potentially poisonous art;
Angels who have shed their wings in the rush to flee despair.

The marketplace:
Dark and deep,
Mysterious well.
Wine of heaven:
Glass from hell.

Peter Pan Meets Captain Hook's Daughters

As night descends the transformation begins: city and soul embrace.

In black leather boots, gold bangles and finery,
A swash-buckling demon cavorts across the stage.
She seizes a pole and spins; cream-colored thighs caress the brass
And spike heels crash against the mirrored floor.
Her glittering eyes suggest tales of vengeance, passion, plunder:
Yo, ho, ho and a bottle of rum!

Meanwhile, the moon stares back silently at screaming electric lights
On streets below.
Hazards abound as a rhythm resounds through a labyrinth of bars and
Oceans of alcohol.

Silk is not as smooth nor as flawless;
A black leather mini-skirt tauntingly, flauntingly (hauntingly!) hints at
The perfect flesh captured within fishnet stockings.
Visions of skin torture the eyes like water rations withheld from the
Parched throats of a thirst-crazed crew lost at sea.
Greedily drink, and the torment intensifies.

Indulgence and redemption: hints of daylight intrude on the pristine
Dreams of the comatose. Images flicker through the mind, transmitting
Dreams within dreams.

Resurrection and relapse are locked together in a treasure chest and buried.
Night has surrendered to the morning calm.
The pirates have sailed away.

Conjugal Karma

Coming home late
In fear of the rolling pin
Doing time in the dog house
For an evening of sin

One might elude the near term
Punishment at hand,
But one never escapes
The wrath of the cosmic frying pan

You can cry, you can wonder why
But you will never escape
The great rolling pin in the sky

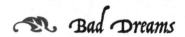 Bad Dreams

Incessant murmurings
Conjure morbid nostalgia
For sad realities that never were.

Lingering fears crawl like insects:
In and out
In and out

Unrelenting darkness screams from the textured perfection of orchids
Cultivated in hell.

I can't resist the urge to pick a flower-
Only to discover I am naked on a busy street
In a city where everybody looks familiar
But I don't know from where.

On the Cutting Room Floor

Our scenes would be steamy
Episodes of passion-soaked
Bliss

Explosives and smoke
Would accompany each
Kiss

But in a darkened room
Behind a heavy door
An unseen and cruel director left our scenes
On the cutting room floor

Queen Emma came for a visit
On a warm summer night.

She spoke without words,
Conveying a message of love.

The Pali Highway was quiet
As I stood at the open screen door
With the moon and the lychee tree basking in royal splendor.

Tahitian Gardenias

Like acoustical shadows in the dark,
A grumpy demon's raspy croon
Echoes through the ramparts
Of a castle on the moon.

On this mid-winter night hot fear chills the air
And reverberates down to the islands below.
While above on the moon
In a warmly-lit room
Lies a woman asleep in a dream.

There's love on her lips, and her hair – dark and full –
Attracts flickers of light to her state of repose.
She dreams in soft colors of flowers rare;
They call out to her eyes and command them to stare.

Her dreams are realities
For the people below;
Her thoughts control destinies
She'll never know.

Tonight in her dream she whispers her will
That the demons of darkness succumb to the light.
In lingering shadows, now sensing their doom,
They turn into Tahitian Gardenias and sullenly bloom.

Black Sugar Mooncakes

Across the waters, far away,
I met a girl.
I didn't plan to fall in love
But I did anyway.

She was an angel
From a town where
Sometimes you see signs in shop windows that read:
"Black Sugar Mooncakes."
Sometimes that's all you need.

She gave me wings and together we traveled through time.

One day I opened my eyes and my angel was gone.
I don't know how long I had been falling.
But I had exchanged my wings for earthly things
And was blind to the transaction.
As my eyes closed for the last time
I saw a sign on yellow paper
Taped to the window of a dusty window pane.
The words were simply put, but they practically screamed:
"Black Sugar Mooncakes"

I could see the door was open
And my angel was inside.
And she held out her arms with a smile and sighed:
"Couldn't you see the sign?"

Butterflies At Dawn

Crepuscular Blue Hour

In rooms of the moon
Somnambulant seasons
Make love to incestuous stars

The night Martian
Carries a rusty ray gun.
He radiates like a tiny blood red sun
With laser-like lightening,
Stabbing the air in all directions.
Who's ass you gonna kick today?

He is getting readings on his monitor: There is a humanoid child, asleep.
His sensors scan her brain waves.
Hearts and flowers rise up in rickshaws of orange and purple.
They want to know: Can you come out and play?

He turns and his sensors register a fuzzy kitty asleep on a furry white rug;
She dreams about how cool it is to lie on top of something
So much like herself and so snug.

His readings have intrigued him and he turns his sensor
To the other, larger female earthling who slumbers nearby.
His monitor scans her thoughts and sees
Silvery green, like droplets of rain upon leaves of a tree.
It is electric in nature, a bit like a siege,
As molecular battles transpire between leaves.
There is riotous color, van Gough and Gauguin.
Chimes in the windows for sale in a can.
When she opens the package, all becomes dark.
For the windows have broken and the chimes will not start.

And then silvery water appears in a stream from the icicle tears
Of a polar bear's dream. And snow melts.
Because the warm breath of hope has permitted the tears
That remained frozen (for so many years) to fall in a patter of tropical rain,
Cleansing the soul and clearing the brain.
The slumbering creature that slept like a brick

Appears alive with emotion and prepares once again for the moment long
Promised. Or is it a trick?

She stirs in her slumber, there are chimes in her ears,
And the steady, loud patter of yesterday's tears.
They drip and they tumble from a sky
Long forgotten, where clouds hover closely but could never be seen.
They signal a death, these warm, cleansing tears.
They signal beginning and easing of fears.
The city of Jade at the end of the night comes alive with promise and light.
Rain falls. Rivers become full. Dams break.
There is a gush of silver in the sky, which collides against the eyes.
In a cool breeze of lavender mist a garden appears.

The night Martian asks himself: why?
Then raises his weapon in the blink of an eye.
Changing the setting from "transport," To "transmogrify,"
He puts the weapon to his head,
Thinks about his homeland -- so cold, hard and red --
Pulls the trigger and enters the dream as a rainbow instead.

Dream Horror Fractal

Write it down
And then
Your dreams cannot hurt you

But what if you are dreaming
When you
Write it down?

The Promise of Shadows

By the light of the moon you feel shadows against your skin.
You pass under tree branches with leaves drenched in silver light.
You feel the texture of your flesh
Illumined in the darkness of night.

A slow flicker provides glimpses of forever.
The juxtaposition of current perception and memory
Move back and forth from present to the timelessness
Of past and possibility.

A sensation that is satisfying and vaguely familiar:
Shadows on skin.
The temperature changes as you move through degrees of darkness and
Light.

The unknown woman walks just ahead,
A mysterious but benign presence:
She has always been near by,
But you did not realize it until now.
She moves out of shadow and disappears.
She is perceptible only in the shade
Of the moonlight.

During re-entry
You transition to forgetfulness.
The whole body tingles
As you transit from dream to dream.

Walking through the house you suddenly feel panic.
You turn on a lamp and it pops with a flash
As the bulb burns out and blinds you:
Leaving you in intensified darkness.

You move through the house and find a light switch
But every object in the house is somehow terrifying.
A cheerleader smiles from the cover of a magazine: Her uniform top says
"Devils."

Everything freaks you out.

A book called "Tiki Style" is lying face down.
From the back cover a woman proffers a bowl with flames rising from it.
She is wearing a grass skirt, a hint of a smile and sinister eyes.
She is surrounded by giant, exotic drinks
Served in mugs depicting ancient gods.
In the background,
The sky is red and the palm fronds are black.

Step out onto the back porch and feel the cool morning air. Look up into
The sky and see the comforting vision of a crescent moon at dawn.

Oh, my fucking God!

It occurs to me that today is December 12, 1873.
I awoke from the recurring nightmare:
I've left the key or forgotten the procedure;
I can't get back
I can't get in
I can't get out

It began on a cool summer night at a garden party on Jupiter Way in
Stuttgart.
The mad scientist mixes an alchemical concoction of strawberries and
Wine.
I somehow find my way home. But not before moving beneath
Streetlights blaring approval as I make my rounds to
Earn my horns.
My hooves traipse through grain and grapes,
Groins and capes -
And the transformation is complete.

And now I search the shadows
Of moonlight
For my guide
To take me back to the state in which the present affords visibility
Into the timelessness of past and possibility.

Meat Sutra

I drifted down to a silent session with an Asian Princess,
And a large black, hairy dog, where we sat at the edge of a pond –
In which swam white, human-length tadpoles
That came to the surface and smiled.

A hand attached to a forearm but nothing more, moved before my eyes
Then picked up a short, but fattened snake, and placed it before me –
A variety of python, I was told.
We were now in a lightly grey room and as time did unfold he displayed
Tiny, distended, square-shaped teeth,
Which protruded as he yawned.

I then found myself chortling among cohorts within the halls of the
White House. We ducked under a table when a warning cry was heard.
But I emerged for some tea or some other thing, and received a blow to the
Back of my head as a flash came through the wall and sent me back to the
Ground. There was a cylindrical hole at the base of my skull
From which nothing drained.
No one said a thing about it, despite the fact the hole remained.

Forays off metaphysical Main Street
Can provide glimpses
Beyond the constraints of our raiment of meat;
And the opportunity to survey the horrific grandeur of infinite seas,
With a high priestess from a hitherto unknown inner-planetary diocese.

Yet the linkage remains elusive:
The means by which saints evolve
By virtue of their robust sins;
As you come to the ineluctable realization
You've become a little too weird,
Even for your friends.

When I leave it all behind,
Become light like a cloud,
No longer wearing a meat shroud;
I want to be there at the jubilee
When that gristle whistle blows.

❧ Ode to Cargo

Death and desire walk hand in hand
Leading us to and from this foreign land.
Live with me and lead me
Electric fan,
Refrigerator,
Bamboo transmitter.
Transform me,
Digitize me,
Mesmerize me,
Supersize me:
John Frum, he come!

Chief Tuk!
I conjure you now.
We walked together among the banyans of Ikukok,
And communed among the stars in the darkness of the kava clearing
And listened to the smoldering howl of Yasur Volcano.
The army will assemble at Sulphur Bay
To greet C-47 cargo planes bearing unspeakable wealth.
The palm trees will sway and the wind will say the greeting of the new
Millennium: A golden time of wealth and prosperity.

The world turned upside down.
Cargo! Cargo!
Mall of America,
Burger King,
Wal-Mart,
H-Mart
My heart, your heart;
Educational transmogrification/
Ritualistic mortification/
Cannibalistic salutation:
Eat me!

And C-47's wing their way overhead,
Circle for a landing
To resurrect the dead.
John Frum: He Come!

I bathe in neon
As I swim among throbbing fish
In a river of humanity on the streets of Shinjuku.
Beacons to the transmitters of desire
Direct me to perform rituals to
Liberate and transform me.
In the city's cacophony
I hear the call of John Frum;
Tom Navy;
Chief Tuk;
Isaak Wan:
I hear your voices in the undulating sounds of industrial machinery;
I hear the belching boom of Yasur Vocano.
Voices in the urban darkness are calling me home....
Home to where I have never been;
Home where I will never rest,
Like a bird in perpetual search of a nest;
Home where a laughing saint
Continues to taunt me
With desire's unceasing jest.
John Frum: I come!

Lament for the Goddess

Thoughts of Calypso On The Journey Home

The spell of the goddess transcends the sea;
As ephemeral clouds in skies of deafening blue
Chant ceaseless reminders she still has you.

This endless stretch of highway is a snake too lazy to turn and twist;
Choosing instead to resist the stimulus of heat and mirage.
From Odessa to points unknown,
I don't know where I'm going
Or how long I've been gone.

The highway's hum makes my mind drift back
To idyllic days on my island prison.
She kneaded me and I needed her.
"Don't try this at home,"
She said with a smile,
And all the while
I drift, further and farther into the night.

Now shrouded in darkness, the highway defies efforts to navigate
The murky maze of my personal haze.
Coursing through the night
The radio regales with tales of heartbreak, betrayal and delight.
And my mind sails away, to the sweet cave of the goddess
To once again play.

Calypso's prison of infinite pleasure
Shared tastes and sensations beyond human measure.
Dark passions awaken, temptations excite;
But the flavors once savored replace earthly light.
Seven years in love's prison I writhed in her grip
And feasted on sweetness of companionship.

She conjured mysteries deep as the ocean.
But all questions succumbed to obsessive devotion.
Her passion presides as ever, it seems
Like a shadow in sunlight from faraway dreams.

As I travel from Odessa to my destination
Aware of my new mortality,
I savor the taste of the goddess again:
Alone on the highway of life's memory.

The sweet music of my captivity is now
Replaced by ceaseless taunts from skies reminding me:
You will never again, yet forever be
A prisoner of love
On an endless sea.

In early November, two roses side by side,
Are glistening in the misty cold.
Yellow and bright against the night
November's Rose is more bold
Than love's own fragrance.

Within the windows of autumn's dream
Lovers lie smoldering in the darkness of a furtive affair.
Candle-light and steam - but not a care -
Fuel passion and desire in ecstasy's lair.

The two roses, by Thanksgiving day
Are now frozen, golden against the snow.
Their beauty encased in a coffin of ice;
By late-November the two have become one,
Enfolded in the soft embrace of a light cluster of accumulated snow.

Their lot is cast, the lovers bond among now-fallen leaves;
The hot-breath of passion cools like the autumn breeze.

By the winter solstice all that is left is a vague hope of rebirth;
One blossom hangs shriveled and lifeless by a broken stem
And one lies broken and brown on the cold ground.

Spring came, but no new blossoms.
Time went by and hope seemed lost;
But one unexpected late-summer day
Hints of two yellow buds returned.

Profound desire teaches how to give,
From profane to sacred as we live.
Love is lust's double-cross:
Satan's albatross.

Juanita in the Moonlight

Shining like a silver mirror
Upon the moment of re-entry
She is the visual reminder of earthly sensory perceptions.

This is the moment you realize you have returned
To a state of forgetfulness and
You say your farewells to spaces you don't remember leaving.

You "wake" to see Juanita in the moonlight and realize
There are those you love who now exist
Only in dreams and memories.

⌇⌇ Sunflower

Pushing up through black, Kansas dirt –
A sunflower seeks the sun beyond the edges of a cobalt sky;
A life, a work in progress; one of many, together:

Standing alone

The end had always seemed far away.
And you were tiny like a seed that might
Or might not come into play.
Now it is the past that seems so distant, as you recall
Visions of our own childhood; eyes by which we saw
How small we were by contrast and in fact.

Lawrence Kansas was your childhood venue,
Its characters your nexus for suffering;
Now neither connected nor contemporary,
They however remain
To feast upon our memories as convivial paragons of pain.

Time brings awareness to sully innocence with fear:
The blameless die while guilty men walk;
Amid agonies of love, and the lack thereof.
And yet it is also time which intervenes for life's vicissitudes to assuage.
We have our principles, to be sure. But we have more than that: we
have age.

With time comes a look of splotched and mottled flesh,
Less the sunflower and more the ancient tree
Which has witnessed the coming and going of generations.
Roots channel deep into the darkness of the earth,
And branches continue to reach for the sky
As if knowing that the final destination is in both directions.

Sunflower!
I am you and you are me

Take a look at your own hands.
You may be surprised to see - as if in a dream or a distant memory –
They are the gnarled roots of our family tree.

Sunflower.
One of many, we are one.
Together, we seek the sun.

Village Idiot

It was midsummer, one thousand years ago,
And the villagers congregated around the Celtic icon.
They offered the golden bough as a sentimental
Testament to the gods of yesteryear.

The priest thought to himself:

I'm in real pain
And I'm really horny.
Painfully horny
To the point of being insane.
Or both.
Or neither.
Oh, never mind.

But my head hurts.
Real bad.
And if I were a toad
I'd be a horny toad.
Or, rather, a "horned toad,"
If you will.

And then the statue began to speak
In a language that only the crazed little girl
(Who everyone laughed at and mocked)
Could understand. She translated the mysterious words.

And the statue spoke
"Skali Ma Kamania.
Kill me.
Kill me.
The voices in the big dream command it."

"Forsake your rivalries and your countenance of frown.
Forgo the forlorn
Be free and fly
Like the birds
And the dragonflies."

"Race into the snow and the surf
For they are one and the same
As are you and the very
Name of your race: the human race."

And the villagers and the vicar all shook their heads
In a collective sigh of disbelief.
It is over now.
And they all went home.
Except the little girl
Who stayed beside the statue
Until she herself turned to stone.

And it is there she continues to stand
In a clearing long forgotten
By a village far-away
Next to a stone statue of an ancient god.

The Golden Bough

Shimmering in the solstice
The golden bough hangs from the rafter that is
Renewal replacing remorse,
Rebirth transcending
The course
Of wayward steps gone by.

Once arrayed in the green and white
Of mistletoe at Yule tide,
The potent sprig
Now wears the wig
Of mid-summer's golden sheen.

Dance to the cadence that causes colors to burn,
As cicadas triumph the summer's return;
Stars are hidden against the brightness of the night sky.
A cool wind blows, as the earth revolves with a sigh,
And whispers its love for the golden bough.

Becoming

To be
Reborn/
Shedding skin/
Redeeming,
Screaming,
Streaming into a new consciousness
And new reality of your own creation.

Corpuscles and brain cells
Convulse,
Constrict and expand;
As growth continues to demand
That you become.

Farewell

Emerging from the cryptic night
The day begins.
I transit thresholds of consciousness to
Depart adorned with ornamental accoutrements;
Wending a trajectory
Through non-linear visions of sound and light.

I engage to complement the order
Within the patterns of chaos
To conjure a muse
Which ignites the fuse and
Burns a rhythm that we may dance.

Inspired by memories of things that never were,
I live them as revealed;
While concealed in moments that unfold
To mold my myths of perception:
Observations;
Incantations;
Contemplations;
Mutations;
Salivations:
Moving with the day toward future incarnations.

Industrial rhythms of daily life produce recurring
Structures of mesmerizing implications.
The constituent elements of the organism
Throb within the larger cosmos
While recalcitrant spheres resist appeals of
Perpetual undulation.

Iterative patterns form, dissolve
And resolve to form again.
I become aware of pulsating
Through a spontaneous nexus
That quickly ceases to be random,
And coagulates to form patterns:
Disjunctive parallels of elegance
And grace.

The conjugal landscapes of nightfall reveal secrets hitherto unknown,
And sprinkle starlight from the bedroom of the cosmos.
I nod
In response to the kindly
Invitation to bathe the newborn infant of my mind in the moonlight
And transit into another world to complete this cycle of consciousness.

Printed in the United States
by Baker & Taylor Publisher Services